COAL DUST

AND

BEVIN BOYS

Memoirs of National Service at Pleasley Colliery, Derbyshire in the 1940s

CHARLES A. WATERFALL

Illustrated by
Tony Heaton, M.Des. R.C.A.

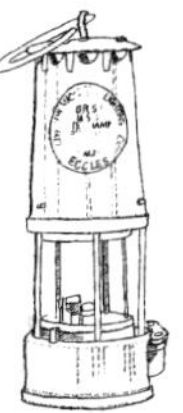

BRIDPORT
AT THE EAST STREET PRESS
2008

The East Street Press
86 East Street, Bridport, Dorset. DT6 3LL

Copyright © Charles A. Waterfall 2008

ISBN 978-1-906746-04-9

The author and publishers are grateful for the diagrams and photographs in this book kindly supplied by Pleasley Pit Trust. Should any copyright have been infringed, the publishers apologize and undertake to rectify the situation as soon as they are notified.

The cover photograph is reproduced by the kind permission of Mr. James Mein, whose father was Colliery Manager at Pleasley from 1924 to 1939.

Best Wishes Charles A. Waterfall

PRINTED IN GREAT BRITAIN
AT THE EAST STREET PRESS, BRIDPORT

CONTENTS

Pleasley Pit
Derbyshire

DEDICATION

THIS BOOK is dedicated to the many men still living and the memory of those who have gone before who were involved with this scheme to help the war effort in the 1940s, not forgetting those who died in accidents or were seriously injured whilst working in the pits at this time.

In March 2008 the Bevin Boys were presented with a badge in recognition and appreciation of all that we did those sixty years ago.

I also dedicate this book to our son, Christopher Waterfall, who died of leukaemia in 1988 at the age of twenty-nine.

Royalties from the sale of this book are to be divided between Leukaemia and Cancer Research in the United Kingdom.

Charles A. Waterfall,
Bridport, Dorset,
2008.

We've reached a point at which there are not enough miners to produce the amount of coal needed to keep the war effort going. We need 720,000 men continuously employed in this industry. This is where you boys come in. Our fighting men will not be able to achieve their purpose unless we get an adequate supply of coal.

None of you would funk a fight with the enemy, and I do not believe it would be said of any of you boys that you failed to respond to the call for coal upon which victory so much depends.

Ernest Bevin, 1943

INTRODUCTION

Ernest Bevin from Winsford on Exmoor, Somerset, was Minister of Labour in the Coalition Government from 1940 to 1945 during the Second World War.

During the latter part of 1943 he introduced a scheme whereby young men registering for National Service were subjected to a ballot if their registration number ended in a certain digit. They were then conscripted to be trained as a coal miner to work in the pits. Other young men who were registering at that time were also encouraged to volunteer for this work

As a result of this scheme 48,000 'Bevin Boys,' as we were called, were trained by experienced miners to work alongside them, helping to produce the coal that was essential for industry, which was working at full stretch leading up to D-Day in June 1944.

This idea came about because of the number of miners who had joined the armed forces during the early years of the war, leading to a shortage of labour for this very important work.

The 'ballot' scheme was not very popular amongst the young men conscripted in this way, as many of them had previously volunteered for different branches of the armed forces.

They were told that if they refused this training to become miners they would be sent to prison.

Pit-pony used for supplies
Tony Heaton

CHAPTER ONE

WEST COUNTRY BOY

ON THE 15th December 1943 I was required to register for my National Service and arrived at Clevedon Labour Exchange during the morning. This Somerset town, situated on the Bristol Channel coast, was my place of birth.

I entered the building, feeling a little apprehensive, not knowing what the next few years might hold for me. As I approached the man standing behind the desk, I noticed a large poster which was pinned on the wall behind him.

Putting my papers on the desk, I said to him, "I wish to volunteer for work in the coal-mines as an alternative to the armed forces" —this was the wording on the poster.

I left the Labour Exchange feeling pleased that I had volunteered for work of national importance at a time when the country needed coal and was desperately short of miners, many of whom had joined the Forces at the beginning of the war.

POSTING

DURING the month of January, 1944, I received my papers, telling me to travel by train on a certain day to Chesterfield in Derbyshire for the commencement of my training as a coal-miner. Enclosed with these papers was a free travel voucher for my journey there.

As I was a volunteer, I became one of the 50,000 or so 'Bevin Boys,' as we were called, who were to be trained by experienced miners to work alongside them producing the coal which the country badly needed at the time leading up to D-Day in 1944.

I travelled to Chesterfield during the middle of February and well remember the crooked spire on the church in the centre of this old Derbyshire town, with its cobbled market square, where we had been instructed to report.

Several hundred men were assembled there, and we were all ushered on to a fleet of East Midland buses and driven to the surrounding villages. I was taken to the Manton Miners' Welfare Hall, near Worksop, Nottinghamshire, where a number of miners' wives were waiting to receive the lodgers they had volunteered to take in.

FIRST LODGING

I WAS chosen to lodge with Mr. & Mrs. Ackerman, who lived at Hardwick Road East, in Manton, together with another Somerset boy from Chard, whose surname was Moon. He was not a strong sort of young man and unfortunately had to be sent home again after a week or two, suffering from heart problems, and did not return. We had been sharing a double bed at the lodging, so after he left I had it all to myself for the remainder of the four-week training period.

Mr. & Mrs. Ackerman were very kind to young Moon and myself and welcomed us into the family circle.

Mr. Ackerman and his daughter were employed at the Manton Brick Works, whilst his wife was kept busy looking after the house, doing our washing and providing our meals.

TRAINING

DURING this time we were picked up each morning and taken to Whitwell Colliery Baths, where we were each issued with a boiler-suit, safety helmet and boots, and then taken on to Creswell Colliery for our training down the mine.

It was a bitterly cold time there in February and March, 1944. Some days, work had to stop at the colliery due to deep snow drifts blocking the railway lines, so we were dropped off at the Miners' Welfare Hall and left to entertain ourselves.

We managed to keep our spirits up by having a sing-song and telling jokes and also by writing nicknames on the side of our helmets with chalk. I ended up with the nickname of Jeff but, although I don't remember how I acquired this, it stuck with me for all of my time working in the pits.

When we first turned up at the pit-top for our training down the mine, we were issued with hand lamps and then sent on to the 'cage' in groups of about twelve. When the cage started to drop, we fell two thousand feet in about sixty seconds, which made our ears pop, but we soon became used to this every time we went down the pit for training and, later, every day we worked at the mine.

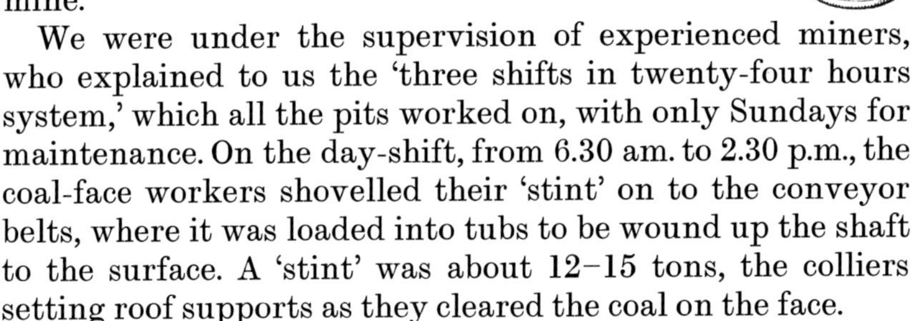

We were under the supervision of experienced miners, who explained to us the 'three shifts in twenty-four hours system,' which all the pits worked on, with only Sundays for maintenance. On the day-shift, from 6.30 am. to 2.30 p.m., the coal-face workers shovelled their 'stint' on to the conveyor belts, where it was loaded into tubs to be wound up the shaft to the surface. A 'stint' was about 12–15 tons, the colliers setting roof supports as they cleared the coal on the face.

On the afternoon-shift, from 2.30 p.m. to 10.30 p.m., the conveyors were moved forward and stone packs were built with rubble to give support behind the coal-face. The back roof supports were then removed to be used again on the next day-shift.

On the night-shift the colliers operated an electric coal cutter. This had a five-foot jib, with a rotating chain which undercut the seam of coal. The machine hauled itself along the two hundred yards of coal-face—a highly skilled and dangerous job, which was done by very experienced miners, who were paid a higher than average wage.

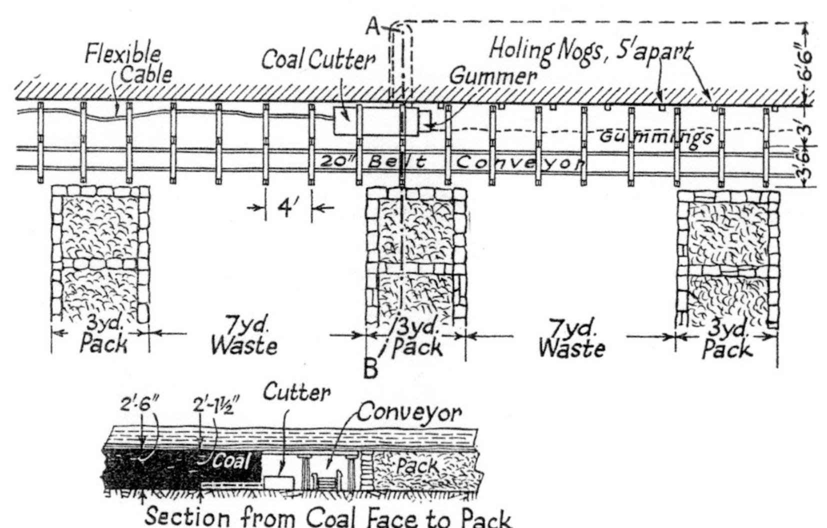

Coal cutting in a 2 ft. 6 in. seam

After finishing each day's instruction, we were brought up to the surface and taken by bus to the baths at Whitwell to get ourselves clean and dressed before being returned to our lodgings.

We could then go into Worksop before the shops closed and spend some of our allowance of about £3. 0s. 0d. a week, which was all we had left after paying thirty-five shillings—

£1. 15s. 0d.—for our lodgings. I remember buying a thick overcoat for £4 from Montague Burton, the tailors, as the weather was bitterly cold.

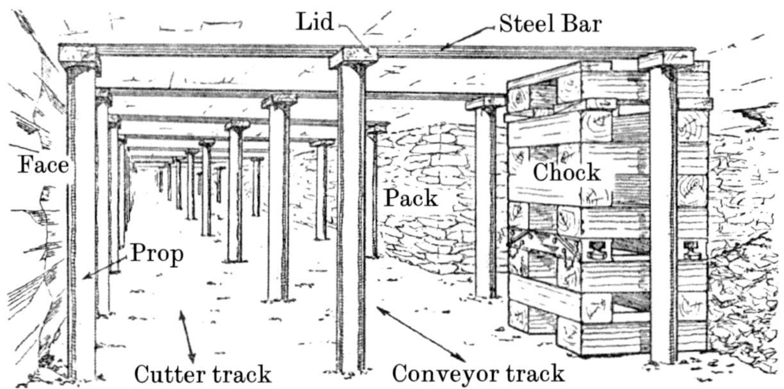

Visiting Worksop was a travelling boxing booth under canvas, where you could have a go with the pro in the ring. If you could knock him down, you won yourself a fiver. One or two of the lads did have a go, but none of them ever won a fiver. I was just content to be entertained at the ringside.

These nights-out were a good opportunity for the lads to relax—like the young Bevin Boy from London who asked me if I would like to have some condoms, which he produced from his wallet, but I politely refused his offer.

CHAPTER TWO

TRANSFER TO PLEASLEY COLLIERY

AT THE end of our four weeks' training at Creswell, we were given papers transferring us to various collieries in the surrounding area. I received papers to go to Pleasley, near Mansfield in Nottinghamshire, for work with the Stanton Ironworks, who owned four collieries in the Mansfield district. Pleasley Pit was just over the border into Derbyshire.

SECOND LODGING

ON ARRIVING there I was given new lodgings with a couple called Jack and Cynthia Mills at Radmanthwaite Colliery Village, which was a new estate built in the 1930s. A typical three-bedroom house was about £500 in those days.

I shared a bedroom with a boy, called Johnny, from London. He had volunteered for the Royal Marines but, because his digit came up in the ballot, he was sent to work in the coal-mines and hated it. Johnny absconded after two weeks at Pleasley and did not return. I never heard what happened to him afterwards.

We were issued with folding camp beds to sleep on in our digs. These were very uncomfortable, but served a purpose as a lot of couples who volunteered to take in Bevin Boys had children of their own.

We were responsible for paying our thirty-five shillings rent or lodging fee, and this was deducted from our wage of

£5 per week. We were welcomed into their home and made to feel as if we were part of the family.

During my three-and-a-half years of National Service in the coal-mines I had a total of five different lodgings. Being treated there as a member of the family was very reassuring for us Bevin Boys. It helped us to integrate into the work-force at the pit, where we were expected to pull our weight, working with and keeping up with experienced miners, who kept a careful eye on us, however, until such time as we were able to look after ourselves.

FREE TIME

SOCIALLY, they were also keen to take us out in the evenings, to get to know us away from work. This made for a happy atmosphere at work and leisure. We soon found out that the local brew, namely, Mansfield Ales, could be, and really was, very potent stuff, which needed to be given the respect it deserved.

The area around Mansfield is ideal for anyone who likes to get out and about, but the only day off we were given was Sunday whilst the war was still going on but, when the pits were nationalised after the war, in 1947, this changed to a five-day week

The Dukeries, Sherwood Forest and the Peak District were all within cycling distance, and were beautiful places to visit during the spring and summer time. Fishing in the lakes and River Trent could be rewarding if you were lucky. It was quite acceptable to take fish home for eating in those days.

Jack and Cynthia Mills had two children, a five-year-old boy, called Johnny, and a sweet little girl, called Patsy. Johnny liked to pick the peas from his Dad's vegetable patch in the back garden, which was kept immaculate. Most miners had allotments, where they could relax in their spare time away from work and provide their families with fresh vegetables, which was a big help, as food was strictly rationed during the 1940s.

When Johnny became ill with polio I had to find myself a new lodging but, fortunately, when I was coming home from the pit one day a lady was leaning over the gate of a house just three doors up from where the Mills family lived.

THIRD LODGING

SHE SAID to me in her broad Derbyshire dialect, "I hear you've to find new lodgings. I'll take you in me duck," and so I moved three houses up the road to lodge with Cynthia's brother, Johnny Bennett, and his wife, Ivy. Again I was made very welcome into their home, where they had a seventeen-year-old daughter called Maggie, who tried hard to make me dance at the local Riverside Ballroom on Saturday nights. I definitely had two left feet in those days, and I had never even heard of the Hokey-Cokey either.

Johnny Bennett was the Overseer at 3's coal-face in the Dunsil seam at Pleasley. Several men on the Radmanthwaite estate worked on this face under his supervision, where they were all paid on a piece-work basis, earning more money than men on the basic pay. I remember that they mostly owned their own houses, as opposed to others who lived in colliery houses and paid rent to the Company.

MORE TRAINING

WHEN WE reported for work on the first day at Pleasley, we were put in the charge of a Mr. Groves, who was the Training Officer for the Stanton Ironworks. We were taken on a bus each day to Bilsthorpe Colliery, which was also owned by the Company.

Bilsthorpe had been involved with a serious pit disaster a few years previously, when a number of miners had died in a flash explosion in one section of the mine. This section was sealed off afterwards and never reopened.

We were given another four weeks' training, being instructed in haulage work. This involved transporting the coal in tubs from the coal-face loader point to the pit-bottom, for winding up to the surface. This cage in the shaft could carry up to eight or more tubs at a time, and when they reached the surface they were emptied by a 'tippler' machine on to the screens.

Here the miners' wives and older men sorted out the pieces of rock and other rubbish from the coal, which was then loaded into railway wagons to be transported to the industrial areas where it was needed. The men on this work earned £5 a week, but the women had a lower wage.

COAL SEAMS

I REMEMBER that the 'Barnsley Bed' or 'Top Hard' seam of coal at Bilsthorpe was about six feet thick in the pit-bottom, and of the very best quality. Several different seams of coal were worked in the pits around the area, namely 'High Hazel,' 'Dunsil,' 'Waterloo' and 'Deep Hard.' Some of these seams were less than four feet in height, and some were as low as two feet, which meant the colliers having to wear knee pads, and sometimes even having to lie on their sides in water to shovel the coal on to the conveyors. Each collier had to clear his 'stint' during the eight-hour shift, setting the roof supports as he cleared the coal.

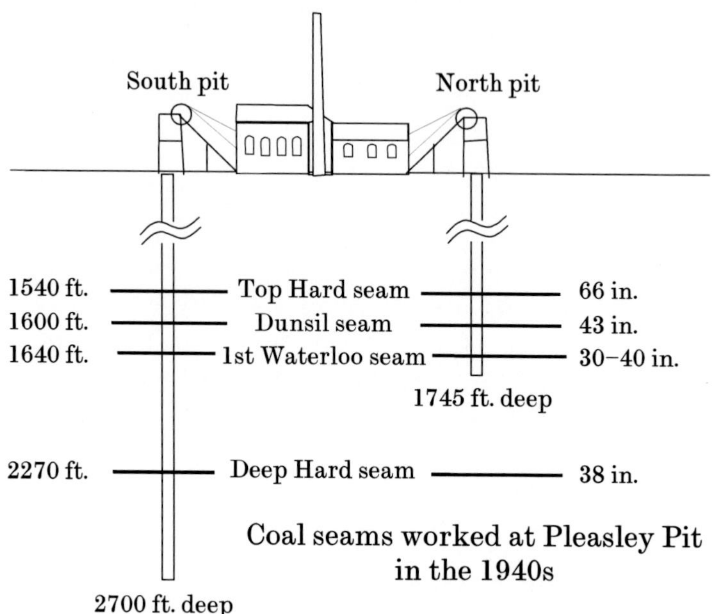

Coal seams worked at Pleasley Pit in the 1940s

North pithead

HAULAGE

THE HAULAGE SYSTEM was based on an endless wire rope running between two tracks. Tubs in 'runs' of about ten were fastened on to the steel rope with heavy clips, of which there were two types. One was called the 'Star,' which you hit with a knob hammer to tighten or loosen, and the other, known as a 'Smallman,' had a handle which you worked up or down, to fasten or loosen.

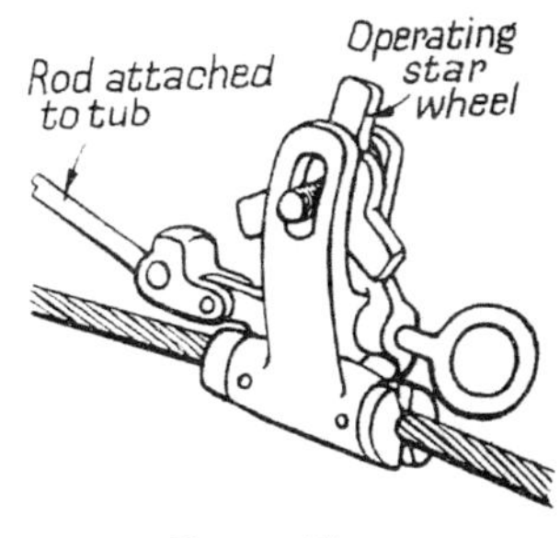

Star clip

Most of the Bevin Boys were employed on this work initially, but some went to work on the coal-faces later. This haulage work could be very dangerous, and you had to have your wits about you all the time with several hundreds of tubs being transported during each shift.

Several Bevin Boys were trained to work at Pleasley, and we soon became friends, although we were always placed separately amongst the experienced miners, once we were working at the colliery.

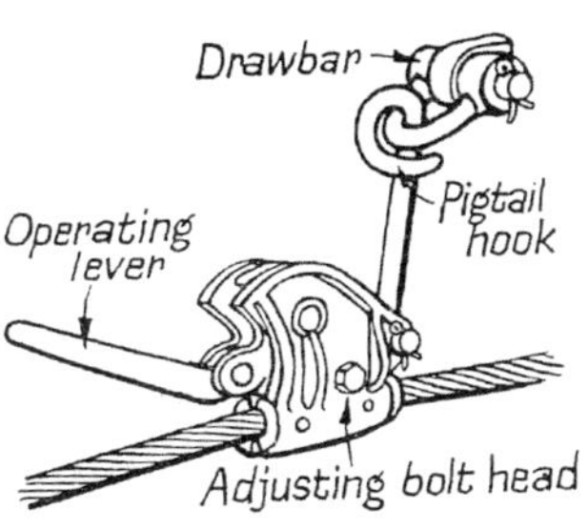

Smallman clip

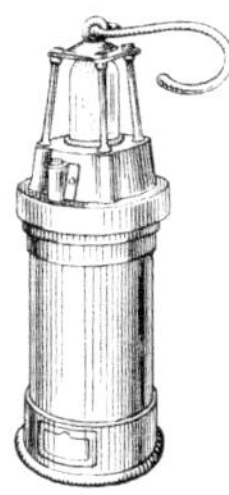

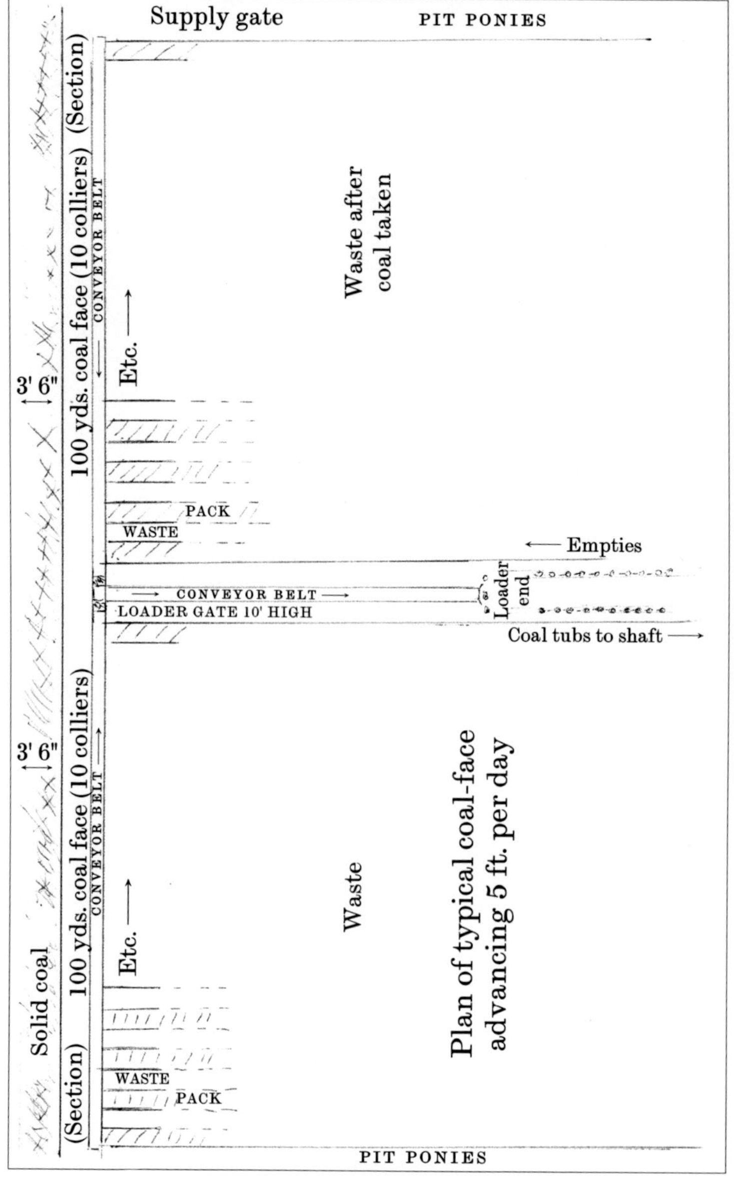

Plan of typical coal-face advancing 5 ft. per day

CHAPTER THREE

SERIOUS STUFF

ONCE we had completed our four weeks' training at Bilsthorpe, we were allocated a works number, mine being 1609, and this number stayed with me for the whole of my three and a half years at Pleasley.

We were also given a lamp number. I was allocated number 83. These lamps were recharged after every shift, when you visited the lamp cabin, going on and off shift. There were also the heavy hand lamps which you hung on your belt whilst working, but these were not used after 1947, when the pits were nationalised. They were then replaced by cap lamps, which were fastened to your safety helmet and were much safer and more efficient.

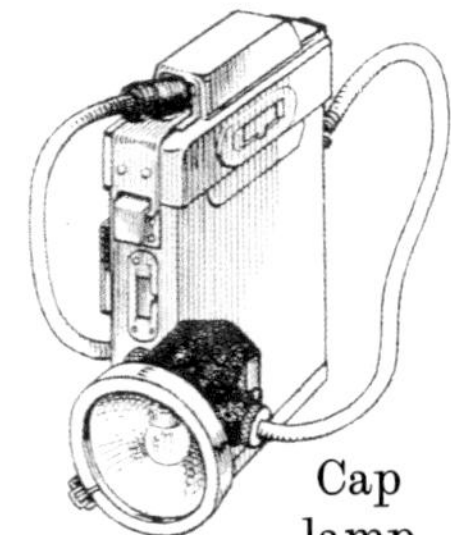

Cap lamp

EARNING MY KEEP

ON MY first proper working day at Pleasley I rose at 5.30 a.m. to catch the green Mansfield Corporation double-decker bus to the colliery. Pleasley had pit-head baths, so you went to your 'clean' locker, for which you were given a key. After putting your clothes in there, and with a bath towel around your waist, you had to walk through the shower area to your 'dirty' side locker and put on your work clothes, safety boots and helmet.

After leaving your towel there for your return after the eight-hour shift, it was on to the lamp cabin for your lamp—the most important piece of your equipment which you

Young miner working on the haulage in the main tunnel
Tony Heaton

virtually guarded with your life. Next stop was the 'cage' at the top of the shaft to wait for the men coming up from the night-shift—looking as black as the coal they had been working in.

We had to be down the pit by 6.30 a.m. in order to walk up to one mile to our place of work for the 7 am. start. I was to be employed on the haulage in the Dunsil seam at No. 3 loader point in the charge of the Overman—Vic Gaunt. It was his job to get the output of the day-shift from 3's coal-face to the pit-bottom in plenty of time for it to be wound up the shaft well before the end of the shift at 2.30 p.m.

Vic was a tall, strong man, about forty-five years old. He was very understanding of the fact that I was new to the job, but also well aware that I had just been trained for the work I was now being employed to do.

It was hard work, and very exacting as there were up to 1,000 full tubs of coal and the same number of empties to be transported back and forth on the two lines of rails in the dimly-lit tunnel. These tubs in 'runs' of ten per run had to be clipped on to the endless wire rope. At times during the middle part of the shift it became very hectic, with no time to relax, as the runs were very close together.

If there was a mishap—which did happen occasionally, you had to stop the haulage rope by bringing the two overhead signal wires together. This rang a bell in the engine house, and the man in charge pressed the 'stop' button. When the problem had been sorted, you rang the bell three times for him to restart the engine.

Vic Gaunt, who was an ex-Coldstream sergeant-major, had the very responsible job of keeping it all running smoothly. If the system was stopped, it resulted in the conveyor belts also stopping, which meant that the colliers on the coal-face would keep piling the coal on to the stationary belt. When the belt started again the coal came twice as fast and thick down the chute at the loader point, filling the tubs in seconds.

LOADING

IT COULD BE—and was—like a madhouse, working there at those busy times. Herbert Charlesworth, the man in charge of loading, wore large, heavy-duty, gauntlet gloves to protect himself from the huge lumps of coal which came crashing down the chute. He had an assistant, who operated a catch lever which let the full tub go and the next empty one come into position under the chute. The air was thick with dust, which stuck all over your body, with the result that you soon looked the same colour as the coal you were loading.

Vic Gaunt would soon let you know if he thought any man was not doing his job correctly, and you soon learnt to respect his orders and keep the system working. Regardless of how hectic it became, you soon became educated in what was referred to as 'pit language,' which included a lot of basic English and French. This language, however, was only used at work.

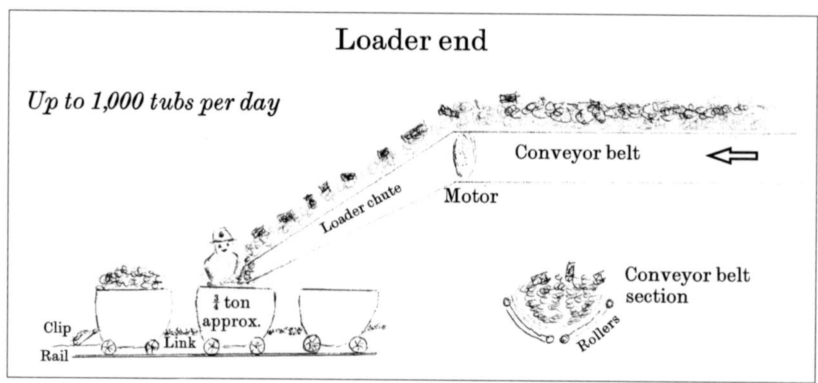

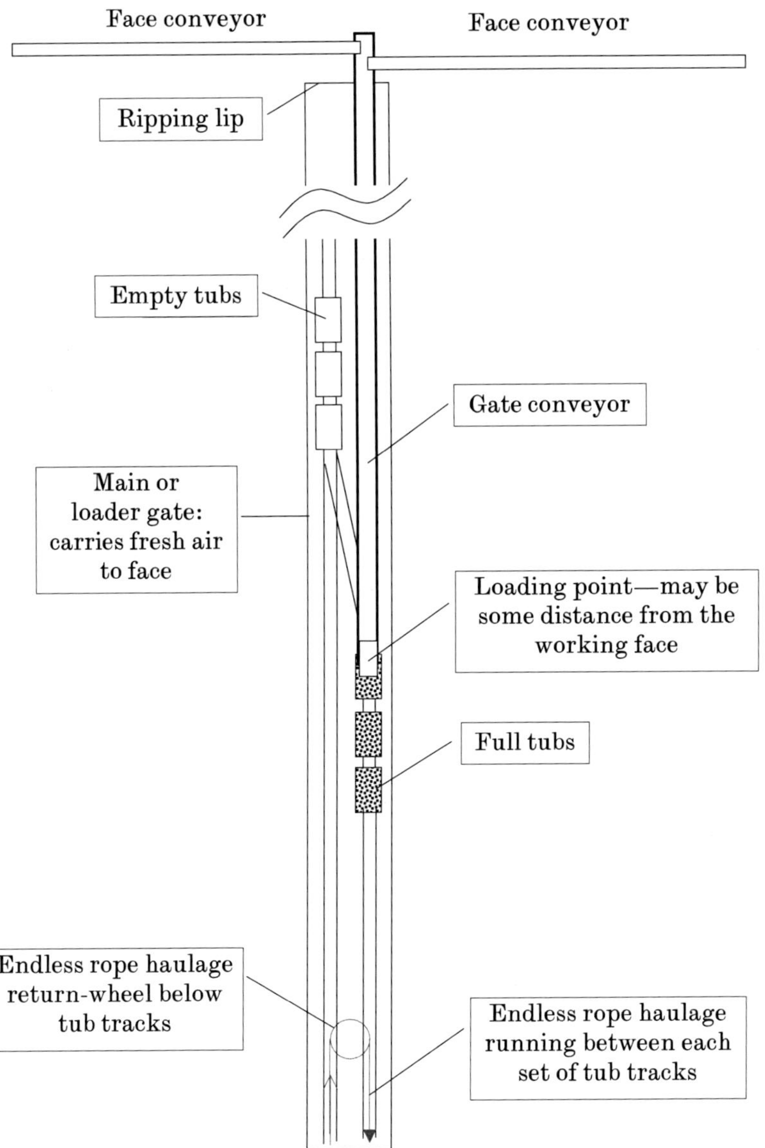
Face conveyor
Face conveyor
Ripping lip
Empty tubs
Gate conveyor
Main or loader gate: carries fresh air to face
Loading point—may be some distance from the working face
Full tubs
Endless rope haulage return-wheel below tub tracks
Endless rope haulage running between each set of tub tracks

Young miners loading tubs

After I had been working on the haulage for a few weeks, I was given the job of working the catch-lever to let the next tub go under the chute. When it was Herbert's 'snap-time,' which only lasted ten minutes, I was given the job of loading the tubs, and when he was off sick for several weeks with chest problems, I was given the job of loading. This was very responsible and quite dangerous work, as huge lumps of coal came crashing down the chute at regular intervals and, even wearing the heavy-duty gloves, you often got caught out by them, resulting in scratches and bruising. The noise was ear-splitting as well.

COLLIERY MANAGER

After I had been doing this job for a few weeks, the Colliery Manager, Mr. Brierley, came on a routine visit to see the coal being loaded. As he stood beside me amidst the noise of the coal crashing down into the tubs, I was told how pleased he was with the way I had settled into the work and that I was a valuable member of the team. From these remarks I assumed that Vic Gaunt was also pleased with me.

OVERTIME

We were given the choice to earn extra money after the hustle and bustle of the coal turning, which ended between 2 and 2.30 pm. When all the dust had settled a bit, two of the older, experienced miners with whom I worked in the team stayed behind to earn overtime by doing track repairs and maintenance.

This gave me a chance really to get to know these men, who had been employed at Pleasley for all of their working lives. They were both in their fifties and lived in nearby villages. I was invited to join them on the following Saturday night for a social drink in Mansfield town and agreed to meet them at eight o'clock.

We had a very enjoyable time together, during which they asked me questions about my background, living in the rural West Country where I came from. However, I was not used to drinking beer and the strong Mansfield Ale soon went to my head. At about 10 p.m. they decided they had better see me safely back to the door of my digs, so it was a good job I had all day on Sunday to recover from this episode.

When doing this overtime track-laying, we were paid 2/3d. per hour—11p. by today's money. This was added to our £5 per week basic pay.

PAY PACKET

The weekly pay packet was worked out by the Wages Clerk, Mr. Coupe. It was his job to collect the 2,000 or so cards from the clocking-in office and have the pay packets ready for collection every Friday, when coming off shift. It was very unusual for any mistakes to be made with the money, which was visible through the transparent envelope—so you could check your money without having to open it.

ACCIDENT

In the autumn of 1944 I had a slight mishap whilst changing a full run of tubs around a junction, taking the clip off, running the tubs around the junction, and clipping it on again to the other steel rope. My leg became trapped under the new rope, and I was dragged along for several yards. Unable to free myself, I had real visions of losing my leg or possibly being killed by the full run of tubs weighing several tons if my foot had become wedged against the wooden sleepers.

Eventually my leg became free again, but this incident resulted in an abscess forming in the leg muscle. I was given a sick note from the pit doctor and was unable to work for four weeks.

FRESH POST

Soon after my return to work I was put in charge of No. 1 loader point in the Dunsil seam. This was not so hectic as the 3 loader station, where I had been working, as the day's output was only about 500 tubs.

The loader end roof was nice and high, with plenty of head room, making it a more comfortable working space. However, a few yards down the tunnel the roof became much lower, being only 4 ft. high. This meant that you had to duck and keep your head down whilst clipping the runs of tubs on to the rope, making the working conditions dangerous.

When Mr. Brierley, the Manager, came on a routine visit during one shift, I pointed this out to him, and suggested that the low part needed altering. He gave me a very stern look and said, "Are you trying to tell me my job young man?" "Not really, sir," I replied, "but it *is* dangerous working under the low area."

He went on his way but, when I came to work on the following Monday morning, it had all been done as I had suggested. This certainly made life easier and safer when working there. It is interesting to record that whilst working in this section, I found several fossilized tree ferns in the shale over the coal seam.

DIFFICULT CONDITIONS

THE DUNSIL SEAM in this part of the colliery was only 2 ft. 6 in. high but, because it was such good quality coal, the men working there had to adapt to these very difficult conditions, sometimes having to lie on their sides in water if there was not enough headroom to kneel as they set their roof supports whilst clearing their 'stint'—usually about 15 tons per man. Jake Gregory was the Overman on the coal-face.

PIECE-WORK

EACH separate coal-face had a contract which was negotiated with the Management by the Overman. The men were paid on a piece-work basis, and this gave them a wage which was well above the basic amount paid to those on an hourly rate. When each collier had completed his stint and set the roof supports to the satisfaction of the men in charge, he was allowed to go up the pit-shaft and home.

Some of the men finished well before the end of their shift, however, and I remember one called Albert Craddock, who would work in a lather of sweat so that he could go home early. Often he would come past us at the loader point, with his face well blackened, as much as two and a half or three hours before the official end of the shift at 2.30 p.m.

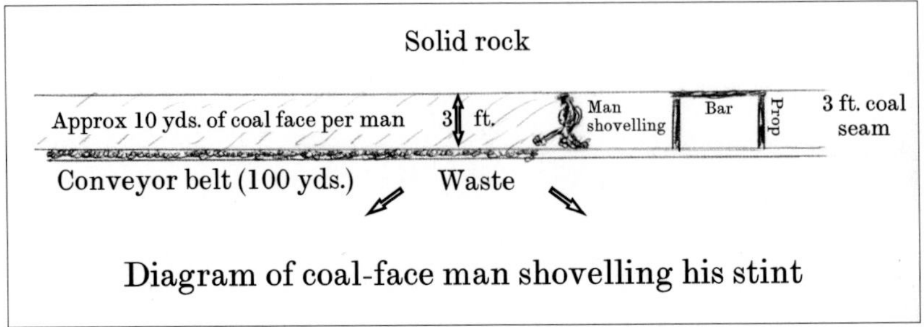

Diagram of coal-face man shovelling his stint

The Overman on this coal-face was Johnny Bennett, with whom I lodged at Radmanthwaite village. He was invalided out of the coal-mines in 1945 with a skin condition, known as dermatitis, which affected some men working in dusty conditions.

Collier clearing his stint on the conveyor
Tony Heaton

NEW OVERMAN ON 3's COAL-FACE

Johnny Bennett was replaced by a younger man, called Cedric Brown, who took over this very responsible job. The coal-face was entering a very dangerous area due to a fault in the seam of coal. Huge blocks of Derbyshire millstone grit were unstable and liable to slip, and there was a fatal accident.

FATALITY

Cedric was dealing with one of these blocks when he was trapped and crushed, suffering fatal injury. All work stopped as his workmates recovered his body and carried him out of the colliery.

This was a tragic example of the very dangerous conditions that all the men were exposed to when working underground on these coal-faces. Cedric was a cousin of the young lady I became engaged to in November 1946 and married in May 1947, four months before my demob from National Service as a Bevin Boy.

SALT OF THE EARTH

During my two years working on the haulage and loader ends in the Dunsil seam I became well acquainted with the men I worked with on a daily basis. They were all a hardworking bunch of local lads and men who lived in the Mansfield area. They were always quick to cover for you if you had a problem, and then you were expected to reciprocate if they had one. We all got on well together.

Some of the names I remember besides Alf Mansfield, Horace Place, Vic Gaunt and Herbert Charlesworth were Keg Alvie, Horace Weston, 'Greeny,' Claude Martin, Bill Froggot (aged 70), Bill Sims (engine driver), Reg Pearson

(Conveyor Belt Overman) Doug Holmes (Electrician) and Lionel Taylor (Overman for the Dunsil seam).

PRIVILEGE

MEN who worked in the coal industry during these times, spanning many decades, were the 'salt of the earth'— always ready to help each other when faced with difficult conditions. I consider it a privilege to have known and worked with so many of them during my National Service time in the coal industry.

'TWIST'

MOST of the miners chewed twist tobacco when working and quite often asked their workmates for a 'twist' if they had run out of their own. "Gimme a chew youth," was the request. The older miners mostly carried a small tin of snuff also, which helped to clear the coal dust out of their nasal passages. Another custom involved the miners coming off shift taking any half-smoked cigarettes from those going on shift when they met at the pit-top.

FOURTH LODGING

IN THE summer of 1945 I had to find myself another lodging and, as I had become friendly with Reg Pearson, the man in charge of conveyor belts at Pleasley, often helping him with his beehives at Radmanthwaite during the summer evenings, he was able to find me a new lodging with his sister-in-law, Dorothy Richardson.

The Richardsons, who had a little girl called Avril, lived at Bull Farm on the main road into Mansfield. Mr. Richardson worked on the night-shifts at Pleasley as a shaft maintenance engineer, and again I was welcomed as one of the family.

I was still working on the haulage, so I had to rise at 5.30 a.m. to have breakfast and catch the bus to the colliery.

LANDLADY

Mrs. Richardson did all my washing and ironing and provided me with two meals a day, as well as packing up my snap tin with sandwiches to take to work, as all my other landladies had done previously.

SNAP-TIME

Snap-time was ten minutes during the eight-hour shift, if you were lucky, eaten on the side of the haulage tunnel and washed down with cold tea out of a bottle, or just some cold water out of your 'duddly,' which was a metal water carrier, filled in from the pit-head bath area on your way to work. It held about three pints of water treated with mineral salts. There were no toilets away from the shaft bottom, so I will leave you to guess how we managed when 'taken short,' which did happen occasionally.

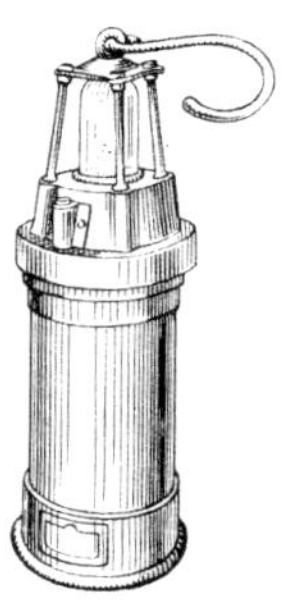

CHAPTER FOUR

COAL-FACE WORK

AT THE beginning of 1946 I decided to volunteer for work on the coal-face. One or two Bevin Boys whom I knew were already employed on the afternoon-shift doing this work, which involved putting up stone packs to support the roof after the coal had been cleared by the colliers on the day-shift.

The steel props and bars also had to be removed as the packs were completed. These roof supports were to be used again on the following day-shift.

UNDER-MANAGER

I MADE an appointment to go and see the Under-Manager, Mr. Towndrow, who was very nice to me, using my nick-name, Jeff, by which I was known to everyone with whom I worked at the pit. He said that I could be employed as a packer and that I was to turn up for the following Monday afternoon-shift, which was 2.30 p.m. to 10.30 p.m.

When I arrived in the pit-bottom at the stated time, I was met by Mr. Shaw, the Overman on afternoons, and was sent to work with experienced miners, Alan Clarke and Bill Scott, both in their 50s, who lived in local villages

RIPPING

THESE MEN had a contract to extend a supply gate on one of the coal-faces in the Waterloo seam. This involved ripping down the shale to a height of about eight feet after the coal had been taken out. As the coal seam was four feet, this left four feet to be removed and loaded into tubs.

Ripping lip

PIT-PONIES

THE TUBS were taken away by the pit-pony, which then brought up supplies in readiness for the next shift. Roof supports consisting of ring-girders were then placed in position, with planks of wood to prevent more shale falling from above. There were supply gates at each end of the 200 yards of coal-face, with the main loader-gate in the centre.

BORING DRILL

I WELL REMEMBER being sent down one side of the face to fetch a 'ram's-head' electric boring machine from the loader gate. This drill weighed about 40 lbs. and it was a difficult task to drag this equipment on my knees, with its cable attached, along the conveyor belt for 100 yards. The drill was needed so that holes could be drilled in the shale, ready for the shot-firer to blast the shale roof down, as it was very solid rock.

Because the miners thought I was taking a long time, one of them shouted down the face, “Come on Jeff, where the hell are you?” When I shouted back, “I’m coming,” the reply came back from them, “So’s f.....g Christmas—for God’s sake hurry it up, can’t you.” I needed all my breath to finish the task, so did not reply to this profanity.

On another shift I was given the job of helping a miner called Walter Wise, a very nice man, who had a contract ‘heading out’ a new coal-face for future working.

HEADING OUT

THIS WAS very heavy work in hot, stuffy conditions, as there was no through air-flow, the temperature being 90–100° F. Work like this was an example of the different ‘contracts’ which skilled miners were able to negotiate with the Management, to open up new faces and increase productivity.

DEEP HARD

ON OTHER SHIFTS I was sent to work in the new pit-bottom of the Deep Hard seam. This was 2,270 feet down below the surface, and new faces were being opened up, also, to increase output from Pleasley Colliery. This again was very hard work in hot, stuffy conditions with a temperature around 100° F. We all carried water duddlies with treated water, but you needed to be careful not to drink too much as it made you sweat a lot and feel ‘floppy.’

MR. SHAW – OVERMAN

AFTER BEING SENT around to different areas as a relief worker for several weeks, I asked Mr. Shaw, the Overman, why I was not being given a job packing on the coal-face, which was what I had volunteered to do. His reply was 'You do what I say, whether you like it or not, as long as I am in charge." When I tried to explain that Mr. Towndrow had promised me I could go packing, he became obnoxious and said, "If you don't like what I told you to do, you had better go home." So I did just that.

ON THE CARPET

THE NEXT DAY, when I reported for work at 2.30 p.m., I was called into Mr. Towndrow's office. He said to me, "Now then Jeff, what's all this I hear about you refusing to do the jobs Mr. Shaw sends you to work at?" When I reminded him that I had volunteered for packing on the coal-face, he replied, "That is quite correct Jeff. You did, and I did promise you that you could be employed on packing. Leave it with me and tomorrow you will be on the face packing, as you are obviously determined not to back down on this."

PACKING

THE NEXT DAY I started work as a member of a team of packers on a face in the Waterloo seam of coal. One of the other members of this team was another Bevin Boy, called Johnny Lines. He was also courting a young lady from the same village as myself. We got on well together, staying in the same team for the rest of our National Service, which ended when we were demobbed in September 1947.

There were several coal-faces in the Waterloo seam, and we worked in pairs—three or four pairs in each team on the different faces. The work was heavy, dangerous and dusty, shovelling the rubble to fill the packs, which were four yards long, five feet deep and three feet high The sides and front were built with large lumps of rock, and each pair had several packs to complete in the eight hour shift.

You also had to remove the roof supports, consisting of metal bars and props, from behind the face, putting them neatly ready for the colliers on the next day-shift to reuse. The coal-faces were turned over by five feet each twenty-four hours, as this was the width of the cutter jib which undercut the 200 yards of face during the night-shift.

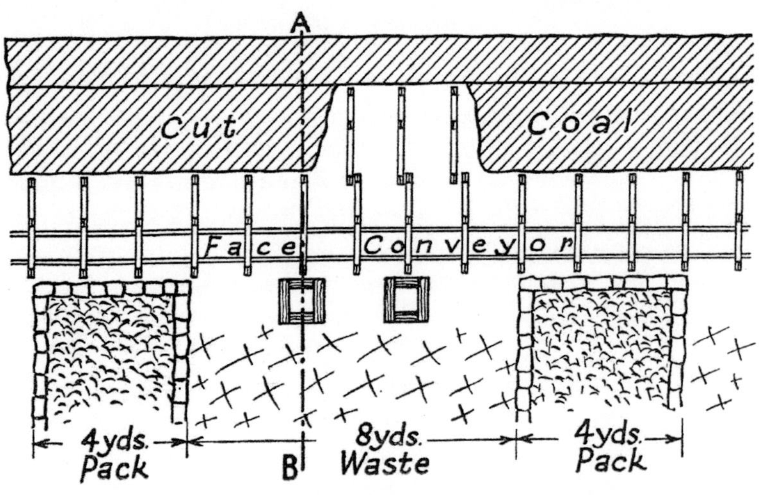

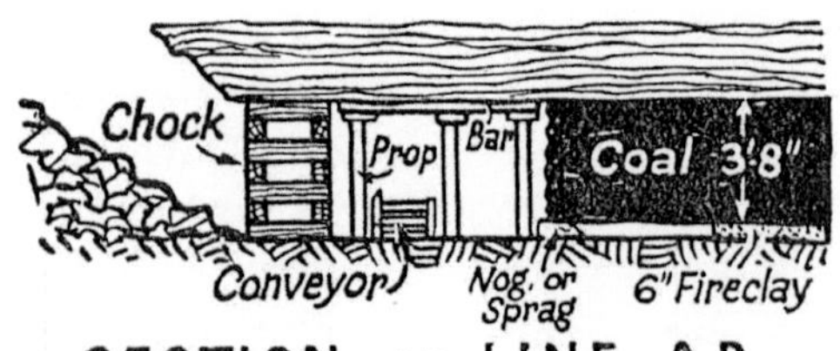

SECTION on LINE AB

RELEASE FROM THE ARMY

One of the men I partnered, when employed as a packer, was Jack North, who had come back from the army especially to work in the coal-mines. This was another scheme which the government introduced to boost the work-force in the pits.

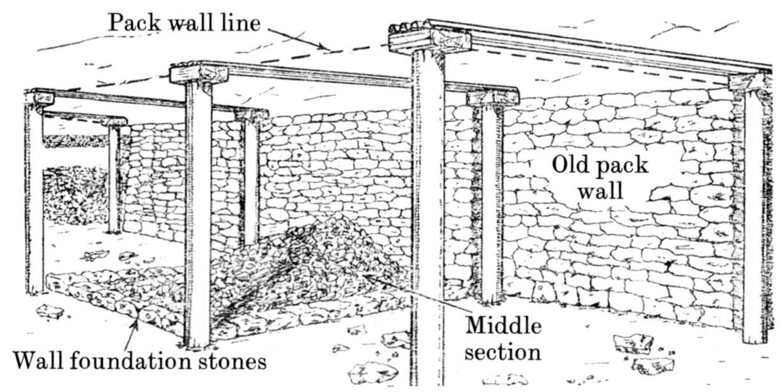

Packing

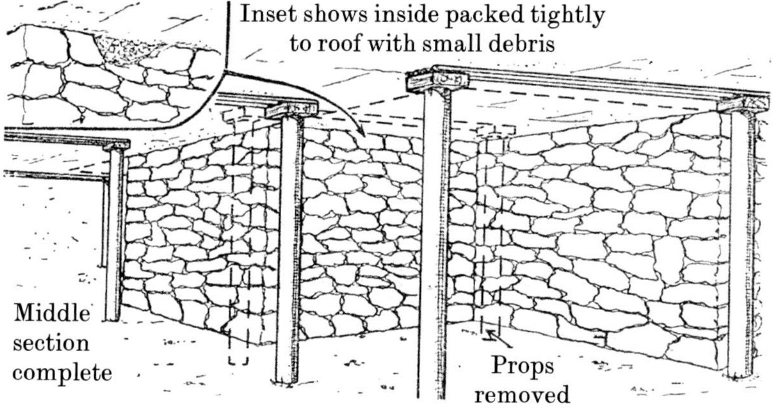

LEG-PULLER

JACK lived at Pleasley Hill village. He was a great leg-puller though, telling me a story about when he was billeted near Loch Ness in Scotland. He and his mates were practising throwing hand grenades into the Loch, when two or three dead young monsters rose to the surface, so they had fresh meat to cook and eat for the next few weeks.

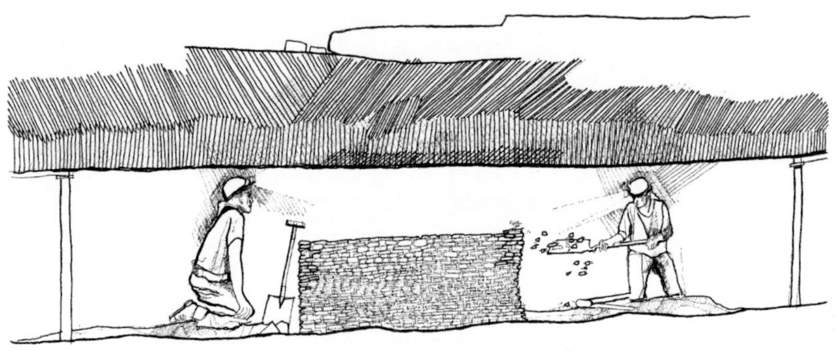

Packing behind the coal-face
Tony Heaton

BRUSSELS SPROUTS

JACK ALSO HAD a vegetable allotment near where he lived and grew fresh vegetables for himself and his neighbours. When I asked him if he grew brussels sprouts, his reply was, with a twinkle in his eye, "Jeff lad, I grow brussels sprouts so huge that when it comes on to rain and I am working there, I can shelter under the leaves without getting wet."

I replied, "Pull the other one Jack; it's got bells on." We both had a good laugh whilst still busily shovelling the shale rubble, with which we were building the packs.

CONTRACT

EACH TEAM of packers had a contract—each man receiving the same pay per shift. This worked out at about £8 per week per man for a five day week, which we were all on after the pits were nationalised in 1947 and the war was over. This was a higher wage than the basic pay.

STRIKE

THE MAN in charge of our team was Harry Blackmore. He decided to ask the Management for more money in 1946. When he was told, "No," he persuaded our team to go on strike for one week. We ended up with a promise of better pay, but we had all lost one week's pay by doing this. The team split up afterwards, with the Overman being replaced. Jack North left Pleasley to work at another colliery near Mansfield, but I was told that he returned to Pleasley later on.

NEW PARTNER

AFTER THAT INCIDENT I had a new partner, Joe Cannon, who lived at New Houghton. Joe was an experienced miner in his late 50s.

ACCIDENT

WE WERE WORKING together one day on 140's coal-face, when Joe noticed that one of the props and bar support did not have a proper wooden wedge, which acted as a cushion between the two metal surfaces. Joe said to me, "We need to be careful here, Jeff, as it might fly out, and the roof looks dangerous." A few minutes later it did fly out as he had feared, and the roof came down, burying Joe under tons of rubble. With only his head showing, I must have looked worried, and he shouted at me, "Don't just sit there, Jeff. For Christ's sake, get me out of here."

So myself and Johnny Lines shovelled like crazy to get Joe clear, which we managed after a few minutes. Joe had a lot of cuts and bruises, and was unable to work for several weeks. This again illustrated how dangerous working on the coal-faces could be, accidents like this occurring without warning .

I had lumps of rock fall on me several times, leaving black scars under the skin when healed.

SORE KNEES

WORKING on these coal-faces for eight hours at a stretch meant being on your knees with knee pads. Even so, your knees became very sore and tender, made worse by the fact that you were sweating in the warm atmosphere. When leaving work at the end of your shift you visited the pit Nurse in the clinic to get surgical spirit to rub in, which helped to harden the skin. After the five-day week was introduced we had two days in which to recover.

DEEP HARD PACKING 2,270 FEET

I REMEMBER well being sent down with my partner to do packing on one of the new coal-faces in the Deep Hard seam for one or two weeks. It was very hot and stuffy down at this lower level. The shale under the seam was very soft, so that the props set by the colliers on their day-shift had sunk down into it, reducing the height in which you had to work down to only about 2 feet 6 inches.

WEIGHT ON

IN THE WASTE AREA behind the face you could hear the roof collapsing with a noise like thunder, which was very disturbing on our first shift there. When I asked one young man who was moving the conveyor pans forward, ready for the next day-shift, if this was normal, his reply was, "When you work down here regularly Jeff, you would soon get used to it," and I laughed. I had not been used to this 'weight coming on,' as they called it. We were glad when we had finished our packing down there in the Deep Hard and had been sent back to our Waterloo seam, 1,000 feet nearer the surface.

VENTILATION

VENTILATION CONTROL was very important to prevent explosions, which could be caused either by pockets of gas collecting in areas where a strong air flow was difficult to achieve or by an excess of coal dust in the air. These problems could be avoided by fitting 'wind control doors' to divert the flow of air into those areas. If an explosion did occur, there would almost certainly be fatal casualties as a result. Stone dust was also spread on the back shifts to dilute the coal dust.

Pleasley Pit was a very well ventilated pit, with no serious incidents of this type occurring during my time working there.

DANGEROUS WORK

ONE of the most dangerous jobs we were given, during our time as packers, was being sent on to a face which had been left without being turned for some considerable time, due to a shortage of men to operate it. When the Management decided they had enough labour to restart this face, they sent a team of four packers and a deputy, myself and Johnny Lines included, to retrieve quantities of roof supports, which had been left for extra safety whilst the face was not working. Because this coal-face had been standing, a thick layer of dust covered everything, and each time you moved or did anything, choking dust was released into the air you were breathing.

MY MATE 'SYLVEST'

We used a ratchet tool called a 'Sylvester,' which had a long chain to retrieve these steel props and bars. The miners had a ditty which you recited whilst using this tool: "My mate, Sylvest, has forty hairs upon his chest." This referred to the cogs on the ratchet and, as you worked the lever to and fro, you recited the verses, some of which were very rude!

It was very dangerous work, because as the Sylvester cleared the props and bars, the roof behind the face came crashing down with a thunderous noise. Fortunately the roof supports immediately next to the face held firm over our heads: otherwise we might not have lived to tell the tale. We were very glad when the job was completed to the satisfaction of the Deputy in charge of us and we were able to leave the coal-face.

The night-shift men then undercut the seam of coal with the cutter, the face then turning over every twenty-four hours. This task which we were given to complete was another example of how dangerous working on these faces could be, as you constantly ran into unexpected incidents during the course of your shift.

SHORTAGE OF RUBBLE.

During one period of packing on one of the other faces in the Waterloo seam it became very difficult to find enough rubble material to complete the packs we were building. In order to get this rubble you needed to crawl down into the waste area to reach it. This situation had come about because

Sylvester

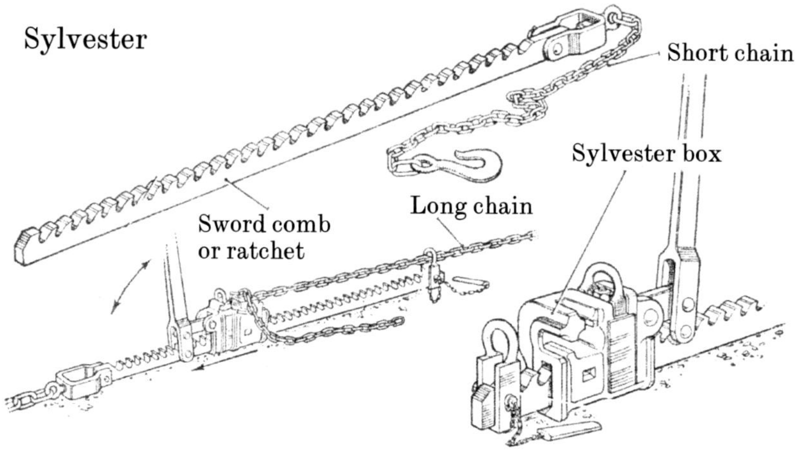

Short chain
Sylvester box
Long chain
Sword comb
or ratchet

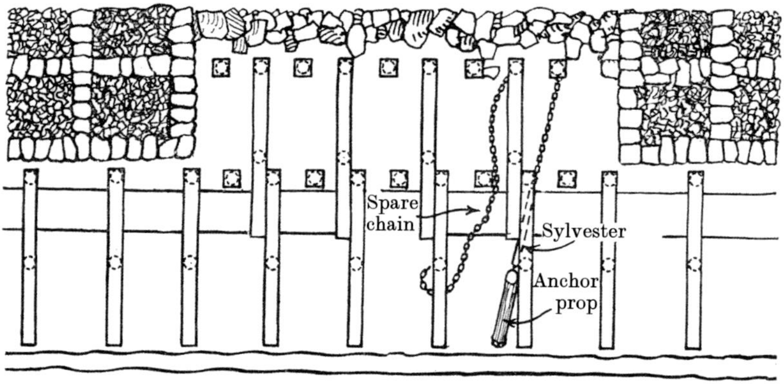

Spare
chain
Sylvester
Anchor
prop

Withdrawing prop with a Sylvester

Anchor prop
Sylvester

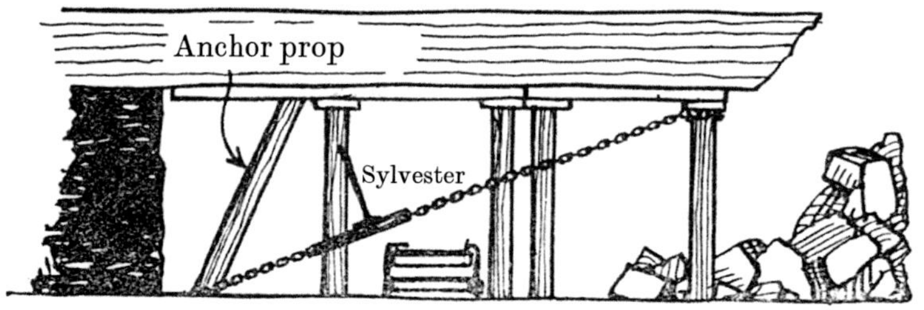

the roof which was left after the coal had gone was very strong and had not fallen.

This was fine from a safety point of view, so we were left with having to use coal off the face in order to complete the packs. In spite of this we were unable to complete them to the satisfaction of Harold Hyde, the Deputy, on his round of inspection.

HOLLOW PACK

HE POKED his Deputy stick into my pack and said, "I'm fining you for hollow packing young man," but when I tried to point out to him the reason he replied, "That's your problem, not mine."

Deputy stick

BCC 47

FINED TEN SHILLINGS

HE THEN ASKED me my name and works number and said "I'm fining you 10/– (50 pence), which will be deducted from your pay."—My pay was only £8 for a week's work. I still keep a Deputy's stick in my porch here in West Dorset to remind me of that day.

FIFTH LODGING

WHEN I had outstayed my welcome lodging with Mr. & Mrs. Richardson at Bull Farm estate and had to find a new lodge, I answered an advertisement in the local newspaper. My new lodging was on Berry Hill Road, Mansfield, with a Mr. & Mrs. Harrison, and I stayed there until my wedding-day in May, 1947. Again, I was made very welcome into their home.

This new lodging was about four miles from Pleasley Colliery, so I had two buses to catch, changing to the Pleasley bus in the centre of Mansfield town.

MANSFIELD TOWN IN THE 1940s

Mansfield, as I remember it in the 1940s, was a thriving market town in the centre of a very rich coal-mining area. It was very busy on market days in the cobbled square, where you could buy anything you needed. It also had large stores like Woolworth's, British Home Stores, Marks & Spencer's, Fifty-Shilling Tailors and Montague Burton, also the usual butchers, bakers and grocers, and shops selling jewellery and hardware.

After so many of the collieries closed after the miners' strike in the 1980s, things were never quite the same; so I have been told by our friends and relations who are still living there.

THE END OF THE SECOND WORLD WAR AND VE-DAY

When the war ended in Europe during the summer of 1945, the whole country had a national VE-Day to celebrate this joyous occasion with street parties and bonfires at night.

CRICKET MATCH

The Bevin Boys at Pleasley were asked to form a cricket team to play Pleasley Miners' Welfare. We did manage to find eleven boys for this match and, when I was asked if I could play cricket, I replied, "Yes, I played in the First Eleven at school," so I was put in to bat first.

When I was given 'out' at the second ball L.B.W., on my walk back to the pavilion, our captain said, "I thought you said you could play cricket Jeff. What went wrong then?" Needless to say I did not have much to say about this and only muttered something about the umpire being a bit short-sighted.

BONFIRE

We lost the match, but we did have a good bonfire on the edge of the recreation field, with plenty of Mansfield beer to quench our thirsty palates. All that was just one day in 1945, but we still had to work down the pit until September 1947.

COLD WINTER

During the winter of 1946–1947 food was still very short with nearly everything still on ration, even potatoes and bread, which meant that Mrs. Harrison had a difficult job in keeping us fed. There were two young children in the family, as well, but fortunately I could get food at the pit canteen, which served substantial meals all day if you needed it.

During this bad winter I remember having to walk into Mansfield in the mornings to catch the bus, as the side roads were all blocked by huge snowdrifts.

MARRIAGE

After my fiancée, Ruth, and I were married in May 1947, I lived with my in-laws, Mr. & Mrs. William Brown in Portland Street, New Houghton Colliery village.

My father-in-law, Bill Brown, as everyone knew him, worked as a miner at Pleasley, opening up new seams and faces, retiring at the age of sixty-seven in 1948. Their three sons also worked at Pleasley during their early years, although Paddy, the youngest one, stayed there for the whole of his working life.

He worked as a collier in the Top Hard seam until retiring at the age of sixty with health problems brought on by working for years in the dusty conditions at the coal-face.

COAL CUTTER

One day, in July 1947, Paddy Brown asked me if I would come to work one Sunday, turning the coal cutter around on the coal-face where he worked every day of the week. It entailed turning this huge machine around so as to leave it ready for the cutter team when they came to work their Sunday night-shift.

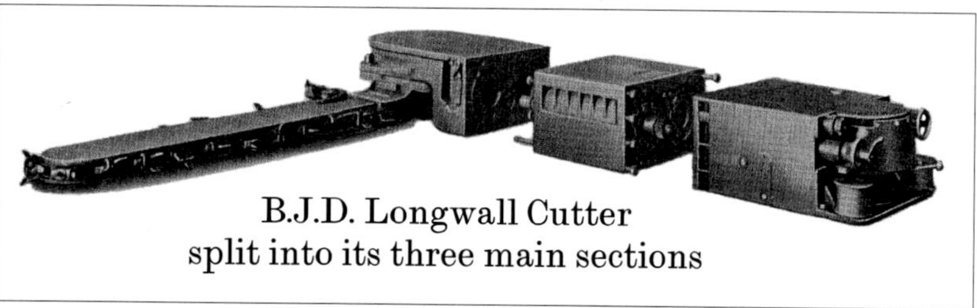

B.J.D. Longwall Cutter
split into its three main sections

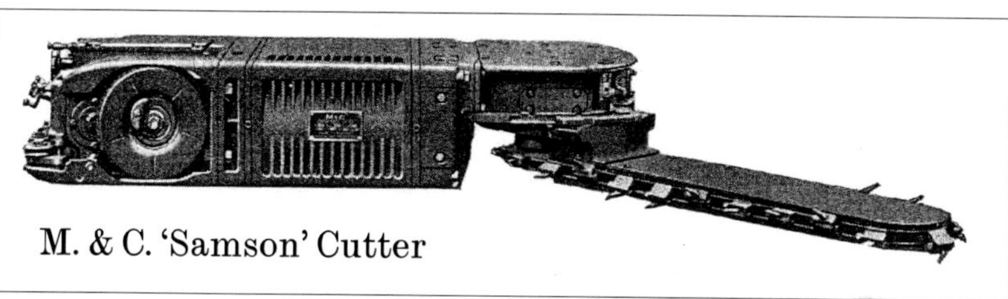

M. & C. 'Samson' Cutter

This cutter was an electrically powered machine, which travelled along the face undercutting the coal seam with its five foot jib for the 200 yards length of face. It had a rotating chain with tungsten-tipped teeth a bit like a chain saw. We duly completed this task in good time to get back up the shaft in time for our Sunday lunch.

BACK WASH

We washed each other's backs in the pit-head shower baths, as it was quite normal for all miners to help each other out when leaving work. "I'll wash your'n if you'll wash mine youth," was the request.

I received nearly as much money for that morning's work as I was being paid for a whole week's packing.

GARDEN : FATHER-IN-LAW

BILL BROWN, like most of the miners with families, had a large allotment where he grew a fine selection of vegetables and flowers, which were all made good use of in the household. I was able to help him on this allotment after Ruth and I were married. He trusted me with this as he knew I had worked on my father's market garden before my National Service.

MOTHER-IN-LAW'S SISTER : PIGS

MRS. EMILY BROWN had a sister who lived in the same street at New Houghton. This industrious lady kept pigs on her allotment during the war years. When a pig was ready for killing, the cry went up and down the street, "Mrs. Brooks is killing a pig."

George Beecroft, the licensed slaughterman, would come up the street, with all his knives hanging from his thick leather belt, and a crowd of young people would gather round Mrs. Brooks's courtyard, which was tiled and drained, to watch him stun and then kill the squealing pig.

He would catch the blood in a container, and this was used to make the traditional Black Pudding. The carcass was then put into a tub of boiling water to scrape all the hairs off. After that he would cut up some parts into joints for roasting and others for curing with saltpetre. Mrs. Brooks would then make pork pies, bath chaps and brawn with the off-cuts.

VILLAGE COMMUNITY

New Houghton was a thriving colliery village in those times with a wonderful community spirit. When the approach roads were blocked by snowdrifts during the cold winters of the 1940s, the colliers would all turn out with their shovels to clear them. Most families knew each other and respected their neighbours, with a lot of them related through marriage.

BEVIN BOY MARRIAGES

Several Bevin Boys employed at Pleasley married New Houghton girls. I remember at least four of us, some taking their young wives back to their homes after our release from National Service, but some stayed on and made a career in mining. Ruth and I still keep in touch with one such couple who live in the Mansfield area.

RELEASE FROM MINING

Ruth and I packed our suitcase and kitbag after my release, travelling down to West Dorset and lodging with my parents until I found out from the Labour Exchange that I was now eligible for the ex-service training scheme for agriculture. I was sent for one year's training on a large estate in the parish of Symondsbury. After my year's training I accepted an offer of full-time employment and stayed for forty-three years.

MINERS' STRIKE

Because we were involved with a coal-mining community, we were naturally very concerned when the miners' strike closed so many collieries during the 1980s. It caused much hardship both during and after the long-drawn-out dispute, and a lot of coal reserves were left untouched at the time.

Maybe, if coal becomes more valuable, some of these might be opened up again.

APPRECIATION

DURING my brief involvement with the coal-mining industry, living and working within a mining community, I developed a great respect and admiration for the men who worked on those coal-faces, whether it was with pick and shovel or the ever increasing use of electric machinery.

Huwood power loader introduced in the late 1940s

In spite of the difficult and dangerous conditions they had to contend with, they had a positive and confident approach to their every working day, with the safety of their workmates always a priority.

It taught me a great deal about my fellow men and left me with a lasting impression, which has benefited me throughout my life.